POEMS OF CONSUMMATION

Vicente Aleixandre

POEMS OF CONSUMMATION

Translated by Stephen Kessler

Boston, MA

The Spanish text is taken from the 1978 Plaza & Janes edition of *Poemas de la consumación,* with the author's dedication to Carlos Bousoño.

Black Widow Press is an imprint of Commonwealth Books, Inc., Boston, MA. Distributed to the trade by NBN (National Book Network) throughout North America, Canada, and the U.K. All Black Widow Press books are printed on acid-free paper, and glued into bindings. Black Widow Press and its logo are registered trademarks of Commonwealth Books, Inc.

Joseph S. Phillips and Susan J. Wood, Ph.D., Publishers
www.blackwidowpress.com

Cover drawing of Vicente Aleixandre by Hollis deLancey
Cover design: Kerrie Kemperman
Typesetting: Kerrie Kemperman

ISBN-13: 978-0-9856122-2-1

Printed in the United States

10 9 8 7 6 5 4 3 2 1

ACKNOWLEDGMENTS

Many of these translations originally appeared, some in slightly different form, in the following periodicals, whose editors are gratefully acknowledged: *Agni, The American Poetry Review, Harvard Review, Mission at Tenth, New American Writing, Or, Osiris, Red Wheelbarrow, Saranac Review, Subtropics,* and *Two Lines Online.*

The translator also wishes to thank Rosemary Balsley and Thomas Genova for digital and editorial assistance.

CONTENTS

IV

V

TRANSLATOR'S PROLOGUE

Passion, Memory and Oblivion

First published in 1968, when the author was seventy, *Poems of Consummation* is Vicente Aleixandre's intimate, philosophic, densely compressed lyric engagement with old age and the mystery of death. The poems are intense, mostly brief, elemental in their imagery (stone, ocean, wind, fire), and they address, in sometimes gnomic terms, the unknowable—mainly the paradoxes of memory: the simultaneous absence and presence of remembered love and the lover no longer living. The voice in these poems anticipates its own posthumousness, and speaks at times as if (and now in fact) from beyond the grave.

The aphoristic aspect of these texts is not in the tradition of the epigram—a zinger of wisdom that neatly sums up an insight or idea—but rather in the elusive sense of an effort to boil down understanding to a koanic riddle, a conceptual contradiction, often in one line or minimalistic sentence ("Not knowing is living. Knowing, dying." "You, my nocturnity made of light, which blinds me."), or in a brief argument, leaving the reader to ponder its resonances. Aleixandre's poems from as early as the late 1920s have a strong sonic element, a rhetorical sense of melody that carries them along on waves of musical language, and these later works carry forward that lyric tendency. But unlike the baroque extravagance of his early masterworks *La destrucción o el amor* (1934) and *Sombra del paraíso* (1944), and the big books of his middle years *Historia del corazón* (1954) and *En un vasto dominio* (1963), here the poet pares away everything inessential in an attempt, in the manner of the pre-Socratic Greeks or the author of the *Tao Teh Ching,* to cut through to some core truth.

For Aleixandre, the most convincing reality, the deepest spiritual and at the same time sensory experience, is physical love. In these poems he reveals how memory, elusive and ineffable as it is, remains the strongest evidence we have of having lived—especially as we face life's end—and the combination of longing and possession it engenders is an unsatisfactory yet also consoling recovery of the lover's lost embrace. The mouth and lips especially, the kiss and the speaking voice, are the means through which we register our richest grasp of life. At the far edge of existence, in the face of death, the remembered kiss and the poet's voice (condemned to mere paper but still singing) redeem what's left of us, even if it is a diminished incarnation of the beauty and vitality of youth.

The combination of passion, despair, solace, resignation and detachment present in almost every poem speaks to the poet's capacity to synthesize incompatible states of mind into an utterance both cogent and without resolution or false hope. These are not feel-good poems with tidy lessons to teach, but open-ended admissions that we can never comprehend the mystery that envelopes the human being. What we *can* do, in this case through spare yet freighted language, is to engage unflinchingly with oblivion on the chance that some trace of us—of our psychosensual selves, our pleasures and sufferings, our gains and losses—may outlive us, testifying to the consummation (both the fulfillment and blazing destruction) of desire.

Born in 1898 in Seville, Aleixandre spent his early years in the Andalusian seaside city of Málaga, where much of the primary imagery in his poetry originates. Sand, waves, ocean, sun, coastal breezes recur in his poems as touchstones of childhood truth. Like Wordsworth, he idealizes and idyllicizes the young boy's memory of the natural world as a lost Eden—a theme explored at length and with great beauty in *Sombra del paraíso (Shadow of Paradise)*. As the youth matures, the vision of Paradise is overlaid on the body of the lover, and the communion with an unspoiled Nature becomes the oneness of the sexual embrace.

In Madrid, where he had come of age and initially studied law, Aleixandre fell in with the cohort of poets and artists known as the Generation of 1927 and soon became one of its leading voices. The civil war, beginning in 1936, was to doom this gifted group to tragedy and exile—Federico García Lorca most famously executed by fascist militia, and others like Pedro Salinas, Rafael Alberti, Luis Cernuda and Jorge Guillén driven abroad for the duration of the forty-year Franco dictatorship—Alberti alone surviving to return to Spain. Aleixandre, due to ill health, remained in the country and became for subsequent generations a living connection with that constellation of extinguished promise and realized genius.

Following in a long tradition of young poets visiting the maestro in the same home on Velintonia Street where his friends had gathered in the thirties, I met Aleixandre in 1973 and stayed in touch with him until shortly before his death eleven years later, translating his poems and visiting him for the last time in 1978. The previous year he had won the Nobel Prize for literature, which disrupted his tranquil domestic life next door to a convent in that Madrid suburb. The Nobel gave him a moment of world fame, even though in Spain and Latin America he had long since been acknowledged as one of the century's most important Spanish-language poets. He remains relatively little known in the United States and other Anglophone countries in part because his poems are especially problematic for translators—presenting daunting challenges in both sense and style—and have seldom been rendered in an English that measures up to the original.

A Longing for the Light, Lewis Hyde's edition of Aleixandre's selected poems in translation, remains the only substantial collection of his verse widely available in the US. Other translations exist, including my selection from *La destrucción o el amor (Destruction or Love),* but most are out of print and hard to come by. This book is an attempt to bring to light a little-known volume of the poet's writing in hopes it may help to raise his visibility in the increasingly abundant landscape of twentieth-century Spanish-language poetry in English.

I have sought in my translations to honor the inherent strangeness of Aleixandre's voice—its sometimes eccentric grammar, its surreal imagery, its ambiguity—trying to retain its often cryptic and paradoxical qualities, while also echoing its sounds and rhythms, as well as its implicit meanings, enigmatic as they may be. The original Spanish is presented on facing pages as a standard against which to measure the reliability of these versions. As with any translation, this one is provisional, but perhaps it will serve the uninitiated as an introduction to the later, highly distinctive work of an extraordinary poet.

—STEPHEN KESSLER

POEMAS DE LA CONSUMACIÓN

POEMS OF CONSUMMATION

I

LAS PALABRAS DEL POETA

Después de las palabras muertas,
de las aún pronunciadas o dichas,
¿qué esperas? Unas hojas volantes,
más papeles dispersos. ¿Quién sabe? Unas palabras
deshechas, como el eco o la luz que muere allá en gran
   noche.

Todo es noche profunda.
Morir es olvidar unas palabras dichas
en momentos de delicia o de ira, de éxtasis o abandono,
cuando, despierta el alma, por los ojos se asoma
más como luz que cual sonido experto.
Experto, pues que dispuesto fuese
en virtud de su son sobre página abierta,
apoyado en palabras, o ellas con el sonido calan
el aire y se reposan. No con virtud suprema,
pero sí con un orden, infalible, si quieren.
Pues obedientes, ellas, las palabras, se atienen
a su virtud y dóciles
se posan soberanas, bajo la luz se asoman
por una lengua humana que a expresarlas se aplica.

Y la mano reduce
su movimiento a hallarlas,
no: a descubrirlas, útil, mientras brillan, revelan,
cuando no, en desengaño, se evaporan.

Así, quedadas a las veces, duermen,
residuo al fin de un fuego intacto
que si murió no olvida,
pero débil su memoria dejó, y allí se hallase.

Todo es noche profunda.
Morir es olvidar palabras, resortes, vidrio, nubes,
para atenerse a un orden
invisible de día, pero cierto en la noche, en gran abismo.

THE POET'S WORDS

After the dead words,
after the ones still said and spoken,
what do you expect? Some flying leaves,
more scattered papers. Who knows? Some dissolving
words, like the light or the echo dying out there in the
great night.

It is all deep night.
To die is to forget some words that were spoken
in moments of pleasure or anger, ecstasy or abandon,
when, the soul awakened, out of the eyes leaps
something more like light than any skilled sound.
Skilled because poised
in the power of its song on a blank page
held up by words, or they with their sound suffusing
the air and settling down. Not any higher power,
but with a certain unfailing order, if you will.
Since they're obedient, these words, they stay
in character and quietly
settle, sovereign, and emerge in the light
of a human tongue applying itself to pronounce them.

And the hand restricts
the way it moves to find them,
no: discover them, useful as long as they shine or reveal,
and if not, disillusioned, they evaporate.

And sometimes they stay that way, asleep,
what's left of a fire
that doesn't forget even though it dies,
its memory enfeebled, but found there.

It is all deep night.
To die is to forget words, springs, glass, clouds,
to abide by an order
invisible all day but certain at night, in the vast emptiness.

Allí la tierra, estricta,
no permite otro amor que el centro entero.
Ni otro beso que serle.
Ni otro amor que el amor que, ahogado, irradia.

En las noches profundas
correspondencia hallasen
las palabras dejadas o dormidas.
En papeles volantes ¿quién las sabe u olvida?
Alguna vez, acaso, resonarán, ¿quién sabe?,
en unos pocos corazones fraternos.

There the earth in its rigor
allows no other love than the all-consuming.
No other kiss than the all-being.
No other love than the love that, drowned, illumines.

In the deepest nights
words left behind or asleep
may find their connections.
In scattered papers, who knows or forgets them?
Someday perhaps they'll resonate—who knows?—
in a few sympathetic hearts.

LOS AÑOS

¿Son los años su peso o son su historia?
Lo que más cuesta es irse
despacio, aún con amor, sonriendo. Y dicen: "Joven;
ah, cuán joven estás..." ¿Estar, no ser? La lengua es justa.
Pasan esas figuras sorprendentes. Porque el ojo—que está
   aún vivo—mira
y copia el oro del cabello, la carne rosa, el blanco del súbito
   marfil. La risa es clara
para todos, y también para él, que vive y óyela.
Pero los años echan
algo como una turbia claridad redonda,
y él marcha en el fanal odiado. Y no es visible
o apenas lo es, porque desconocido pasa, y sigue envuelto.

No es posible romper el vidrio o el aire
redondos, ese cono perpetuo que es algo alberga:
aún un ser que se mueve y pasa, ya invisible.
Mientras los otros, libres, cruzan, ciegan.

Porque cegar es emitir su vida en rayos frescos.
Pero quien pasa a solas, protegido
por su edad, cruza sin ser sentido. El aire, inmóvil.

Él oye y siente, porque el muro extraño
roba a él la luz pero aire es sólo
para la luz que llega, y pasa el filo.
Pasada el alma, en pie, cruza aún quien vive.

THE YEARS

Do the years add up to their weight or to their story?
What costs most is to go away
slowly, still full of love, smiling. And they say, "Young;
ah, how young you are..." Are, not were? The tense is
  true.
Those figures pass, full of surprises. Because the eye—
  which is still alive—looks
and reflects the golden hair, the rosy skin, the sudden ivory
  whiteness. Laughter is bright
for everyone, and also for him, who is alive to hear it.
But the years cast
something like a murky round brightness
and he walks out into the hated spotlight. And he's not
  visible
or is just barely, because he goes by unknown, and goes on,
  shrouded.

It's impossible to break the round glass
or the air, that perpetual cone sheltering something:
even a being who moves and goes by, invisible.
While the rest pass freely, blindingly.

Because to bedazzle is to shed your life in fresh rays of light.
But whoever goes by alone, protected
by his age, passes without a trace. The air unmoved.

He sees and he feels, because the strange wall
steals his light, but air is only
for light that crosses the line.
The soul gone on, upright, keeps crossing paths with
  whoever is alive.

LOS VIEJOS Y LOS JÓVENES

Unos, jóvenes, pasan. Ahí pasan, sucesivos,
ajenos a la tarde gloriosa que los unge.
Como esos viejos
más lentos van uncidos
a ese rayo final del sol poniente.
Éstos sí son conscientes de la tibieza de la tarde fina.
Delgado el sol les toca y ellos toman
su templanza: es un bien—¡quedan tan pocos!—,
y pasan despaciosos por esa senda clara.

Es el verdor primero de la estación temprana.
Un río juvenil, más bien niñez de un manantial cercano,
y el verdor incipiente: robles tiernos,
bosque hacia el puerto en ascensión ligera.
Ligerísima. Mas no van ya los viejos a su ritmo.
Y allí los jóvenes que se adelantan pasan
sin ver, y siguen, sin mirarles.
Los ancianos los miran. Son estables,
éstos, los que al extremo de la vida,
en el borde del fin, quedan suspensos,
sin caer, cual por siempre.
Mientras las juveniles sombras pasan, ellos sí, consumibles,
  inestables,
urgidos de la sed que un soplo sacia.

THE OLD AND THE YOUNG

Some people, young, are passing. There they go, one after
  another,
strangers to the glorious afternoon anointing them.
As those old ones
go more slowly, yoked
to that last ray of the setting sun.
They're fully aware of the warmth of the fine afternoon.
Lightly the sun touches them and they drink in
its mildness: it's a gift—so few are left!—
and they move slowly down that well lit path.

It's the first green of the new season.
A young river, more like the childhood of a nearby stream,
and the budding green: delicate oaks,
woods floating weightless down to the port.
So light. But the old don't move to that rhythm anymore.
And there the young moving along pass by
not even seeing, and move on, not noticing.
The old ones notice. They're stable,
these people at the far end of life,
at the edge of the end, who stay suspended,
without falling, as if forever.
While the young shadows pass, they do, consumable,
  unstable,
urged on by a thirst that's quenched by a gust of wind.

COMO MOISÉS ES EL VIEJO

Como Moisés en lo alto del monte.

Cada hombre puede ser aquél
y mover la palabra y alzar los brazos
y sentir cómo barre la luz, de su rostro,
el polvo viejo de los caminos.

Porque allí está la puesta.
Mira hacia atrás: el alba.
Adelante: más sombras. ¡Y apuntaban las luces!
Y él agita los brazos y proclama la vida,
desde su muerte a solas.

Porque como Moisés, muere.
No con las tablas vanas y el punzón, y el rayo en las alturas,
sino rotos los textos en la tierra, ardidos
los cabellos, quemados los oídos por las palabras terribles,
y aún aliento en los ojos, y en el pulmón la llama,
y en la boca la luz.

Para morir basta un ocaso.
Una porción de sombra en la raya del horizonte.
Un hormiguear de juventudes, esperanzas, voces.
Y allá la sucesión, la tierra: el límite.
Lo que verán los otros.

THE OLD MAN IS LIKE MOSES

Like Moses on the mountaintop.

Every man can be like him
and say the words and raise his arms
and feel the way the light sweeps the dust
of the old roads off his face.

Because there's the sunset.
He looks back: dawn.
Ahead: more shadows. And the lights coming on.
And he waves his arms and declares for life
out of his solitary death.

Because like Moses, he's dying.
Not with the smashing of tablets and the lightning flash,
but with the broken texts on the ground, his hair
ashen, his ears scorched by the terrible words,
and still some breath in his eyes, some fire in his lungs,
some light in his mouth.

One sunset is all it takes to die.
Just a sliver of shadow along the horizon.
A swarm of young times, voices, hopes.
And over there what follows, the earth: the limit.
What the others will see.

HORAS SESGAS

Durante algunos años fui diferente,
o fui el mismo. Evoqué principados, viles ejecutorias
o victoria sin par. Tristeza siempre.
Amé a quienes no quise. Y desamé a quien tuve.
Muralla fuera el mar, quizá puente ligero.
No sé si me conocí o si aprendí a ignorarme.
Si respeté a los peces, plata viva en las horas,
o intenté domeñar a la luz. Aquí palabras muertas.
Me levanté con enardecimiento, callé con sombra, y tarde.
Ávidamente ardí. Canté ceniza.
Y si metí en el agua un rostro no me reconocí. Narciso es
  triste.
Referí circunstancia. Imprequé a las esferas
y serví la materia de su música vana
con ademán intenso, sin saber si existía.
Entre las multitudes quise beber su sombra
como quien bebe el agua de un desierto engañoso.
Palmeras… Sí, yo canto… Pero nadie escuchaba.
Las dunas, las arenas palpitaban sin sueño.
Falaz escucho a veces una sombra corriendo
por un cuerpo creído. O escupo a solas. "Quémate."
Pero yo no me quemo. Dormir, dormir… ¡Ah! "Acábate."

TIMEBENDS

For a few years there I was different,
or I was the same. I called forth princedoms, vile pedigrees,
peerless victories. Sadness always.
I loved those I didn't love. And disloved whoever I had.
The sea was a wall, or maybe a light bridge.
I don't know whether I knew myself or learned to leave
  myself in the dark.
Whether I respected fish, live silver in time,
or attempted to tame light. Dead words here.
I awoke on fire, I went quiet in the shade, and late.
I burned with passion. I sang ashes.
And when I saw my face in the water it was unfamiliar.
  Narcissus is sad.
I reported what happened. I cursed the spheres
and served the stuff of their vain music
with intense attitude, not knowing if I existed.
Amid the crowds I tried to drink their shadow
like one who drinks the water in a false desert.
Palm trees… Yes, I'm singing… But no one listened.
The dunes, the sands rippled sleeplessly.
Falsely sometimes I hear a shadow running
over a believed-in body. Or I spit to myself. "Burn."
But I don't burn. Sleep, to sleep… Ah! "Enough with
  you."

ROSTRO FINAL

La decadencia añade verdad, pero no halaga.
Ah, la vicisitud
no se cancelará, pues es el tiempo.
Mas, sí su doloroso error, su poso triste. Más bien en torva
imagen,
su residuo imprimido: allí el horror sin máscara.
Pues no es el viejo la máscara, sino otra desnudez impúdica;
más allá de la piel se está asomando,
sin dignidad. Desorden: no es un rostro el que vemos.
Por eso, cuando el viejo exhibe su hilarante visión se ve
entre rejas,
degradado, el recuerdo de algún vivir, y asoma
la afilada nariz, comida o roída, el pelo quedo,
estopa, la gota turbia que hace el ojo, y el hueco o sima
donde estuvo la boca y falta. Allí una herida
seca aún se abre y remeda algún son: un fuelle triste.
Con los garfios cogidos a los hierros, mascúllanse
sonidos rotos por unos dientes grandes, amarillos,
que de otra especie son, si existen. Ya no humanos.
Allí tras ese rostro un grito queda, un alarido
suspenso, la gesticulación sin tiempo…
Y allí entre hierros vemos la mentira final. La ya no vida.

FINAL FACE

Decline adds truth, but it doesn't flatter.
Alas, vicissitude
will not be canceled, as it is time.
But yes, its painful error, its sad sentiment. Better its grim image,
its printed residue: the horror unmasked.
Because the old man isn't the mask, but some other brazen nakedness;
it's coming up through the skin,
undignified. Breakdown: it's not a face we're seeing.
That's why, when the old man reveals his comical vision you can see through the bars,
degraded, the memory of some kind of living, and the sharp nose
sticks out, eaten or gnawed away, soft hair,
eyes shedding turbid burlap tears, and the hole or chasm
where the mouth was, and is missing. There a dry
wound opens and mimics some sound: a sad wheeze.
With their hooks linked to the bars, broken sounds
are muttered through big yellow teeth,
teeth of some other species, if they exist. No longer human.
There behind that face lingers a cry, a held-back
howl, a timeless grimace…
And there between the bars we see the final lie. Life-no-longer.

II

EL PASADO: "VILLA PURA"

Aquí en la casa chica,
tres árboles delante, la puerta en pie, el sonido:
todo persiste, o muerto,
cuando cruzo. Me acuerdo: "Villa Pura".
Pura de qué; del viento.
Aquí ese niño puso
en pie el temblor. Aquí miró la arena muerta,
el barro como un guante,
la luz como sus pálidas mejillas
y el oro viejo dando
en el cabello un beso
sin ayer. Hoy, mañana.
Las hojas han caído, o de la tierra al árbol
subieron hoy
y aún fingen
pasión, estar, rumor. Y cruzo
y no dan sombra,
pues que son. Y no hay humo.

Velar. Vivir. No
puedo,
no debo
recordar. Nada vive. Telón que el viento mueve
sin existir. Y callo.

THE PAST: "VILLA PURA"

Here at the little house,
three trees in front, the door upright, the sound:
it all endures, or is dead,
when I go by. I remember: "Villa Pura."
What kind of pure—wind.
This is where that boy's
trembling began. Here's where he saw
the dead sand,
the mud like a glove,
the light with its pale cheeks
and the old gold kissing
our hair, a kiss
with no yesterday. Today, tomorrow.
The leaves fall, or they rose today from the ground
to the tree
and still pretend
to passion, being, sounds. And I pass
and they give no shade,
since they are. And there's no smoke.

To stay awake. To be alive. I
can't,
I mustn't
remember. Nothing lives. A curtain the wind moves
without existing. And I say nothing.

COMO LA MAR, LOS BESOS

No importan los emblemas
ni las vanas palabras que son un soplo sólo.
Importa el eco de lo que oí y escucho.
Tu voz, que muerta vive, como yo que al pasar
aquí aún te hablo.

Eras más consistente,
más duradera, no porque te besase,
ni porque en ti asiera firme a la existencia.
Sino porque como la mar
después que arena invade temerosa se ahonda.
En verdes o en espumas la mar, feliz, se aleja.
Como ella fue y volvió tú nunca vuelves.

Quizá porque, rodada
sobre playa sin fin, no pude hallarte.
La huella de tu espuma,
cuando el agua se va, queda en los bordes.

Sólo bordes encuentro. Sólo el filo de voz que en mí
quedara.
Como un alga tus besos.
Mágicos en la luz, pues muertos tornan.

KISSES ARE LIKE THE OCEAN

Symbols don't matter
nor the vain words that are only a breath.
What matters is an echo of what I heard and hear.
Your voice, still alive though dead, like me still speaking
to you here in passing.

You were more substantial,
more lasting, not because you were kissed,
nor because kisses burned you more firmly into existence.
But because the ocean,
after its fearful rush on the sand, grows deeper.
In greens or in foamy whites the ocean happily retreats.
As it fled and returns, you never return.

Perhaps because I couldn't
find you rolling along the endless beach.
The track of your foam,
when the tide pulls back, stays at the edges.

I find only edges. Only the edge of a voice that's left in me.
Your kisses like strands of seaweed.
Magic in the light, then they turn away, dead.

VISIÓN JUVENIL DESDE OTROS AÑOS

Al nacer se prodigan
las palabras que dicen muerte, asombro.
Como entre dos sonidos, hay un beso o un murmullo.
Conocer es reír, y el alba ríe.

Ríe, pues la tierra es un pecho que convulsivo late.
Carcajada total que no es son, pero vida,
pero luces que exhala
algo, un pecho: el planeta.

Es un cuerpo gozoso.
No importa lo que él lleva,
mas su inmenso latir por el espacio.
Como un niño flotando, como un niño en la dicha.
Así el joven miró y vio el mundo, libre.

Quizás entre dos besos,
quizás al seno de un beso:
Tal sintió entre dos labios.
Era un fresco reír, de él o del mundo.

Pero el mundo perdura,
no entre dos labios sólo: el beso acaba.
Pero el mundo rodando,
libre, sí, es cual un beso,
aún después que aquél muere.

VISION OF YOUTH AS SEEN FROM OTHER YEARS

Once you are born the words
are squandered, saying death, astonishment.
As between two sounds, there's a kiss or a whisper.
To know is to laugh, and dawn laughs.

It laughs, since the earth is a beating heart having a fit.
A fit of laughter that's not a sound but life,
but lights exhaled
by something, a heart: the planet.

It's a body in pleasure.
What it's wearing doesn't matter,
only its great heartbeat pulsing through space.
Like a child floating, like a child swimming in happiness.
That's how the young man looked and saw the world, free.

Perhaps between two kisses,
perhaps at the breast of a kiss:
that's how it felt between two lips.
It was a fresh laugh, his or the world's.

But the world goes on,
not just between two lips: the kiss concludes.
But the world rolling along,
free, yes, it's like a kiss,
even when the kiss is dead and gone.

UNAS POCAS PALABRAS

Unas pocas palabras
en tu oído diría. Poca es la fe de un hombre incierto.
Vivir mucho es oscuro, y de pronto saber no es conocerse.
Pero aún así diría. Pues mis ojos repiten lo que copian:
tu belleza, tu nombre, el son del río, el bosque, el alma a
solas.

Todo lo vio y lo tienen. Eso dicen los ojos.
A quien los ve responden. Pero nunca preguntan.
Porque si sucesivamente van tomando
de la luz el color, del oro el cieno
y de todo el sabor del poso lúcido,
no desconocen besos, ni rumores, ni aromas;
han visto árboles grandes, murmullos silenciosos,
hogueras apagadas, ascuas, venas, ceniza,
y el mar, el mar al fondo, con sus lentas espinas,
restos de cuerpos bellos, que las playas devuelven.

Unas pocas palabras, mientras alguien callase;
las del viento en las hojas, mientras beso tus labios.
Unas claras palabras, mientras duermo en tu seno.
Suena el agua en la piedra. Mientras, quieto, estoy muerto.

A FEW WORDS

I would say a few words
in your ear. A doubtful man has little faith.
Live a long time and it gets dark, and suddenly you know
you don't know yourself.
But I'd say them even so. Since my eyes repeat what they
take in:
your beauty, your name, the river's sound, the woods, the
soul on its own.

They saw and they hold everything. That's what the eyes
say.
They answer whoever sees them. But they never ask.
Because if they take in one after another
the color from light, the mud from gold
and the lucid sediment of every flavor,
they never unknow kisses, whispers, smells;
they've seen big trees, quiet murmurs,
dead fires, live embers, veins, ashes,
and the sea, the sea in the background, with its long thorns,
beautiful bodies' remains, given back by the beach.

A few words, while someone is silent;
those of the wind in the leaves, while I kiss your lips.
A few clear words, while I sleep on your breast.
Water sounds against rock. While, quiet, I'm dead.

POR FIN

Una palabra más, y sonaba imprecisa.
Un eco algunas veces como pronta canción.
Otras se encendía como la yesca.
A veces tenía el sonido de los árboles grandes en la sombra.
Batir de alas extensas: águilas, promociones, palpitaciones,
tronos.
Después, más altas, luces.

Más luces o la súbita sombra.
El sonido disperso y el silencio del mundo.
La desolación
de la oquedad sin bordes.

Y de pronto, la postrera palabra,
la caricia del agua en la boca sedienta,
o era la gota suave sobre los ojos ciegos,
quemados por la vida y sus lumbres.

Ah, cuánta paz, el sueño.

AT LAST

One more word, and it didn't ring clear.
An echo sometimes like a brief song.
Others went up like tinder.
At times it sounded shady, like big trees.
Beating of long wings: eagles, promotions, palpitations,
   thrones.
Later, higher up, lights.

More lights or sudden darkness.
The spreading sound or the world's silence.
The desolation
of boundless hollowness.

And suddenly, the last word,
water's caress in a thirsty mouth,
or those soothing drops into blind eyes,
burned by life and its brilliance.

Ah, so peaceful, sleep.

CUMPLE

I

La juventud promete y ella cumple.
Ah cuán larga palabra. Viento en hojas.
Cumple, pero invisible. Brisa en humos.
La juventud promete. (Dura. Duerme.)
¡Cuán despierta en la noche!
Pero ya no amanece.

II

Cuando se ve y se oye, se ha vivido.
Un beso, una pura palabra. Un son. Dos formas.
Un mundo o bulto insigne. Aquí las manos.
Tienta. Tienta o besa. Has dormido.
Pero nunca despiertes.

III

No es tarde. Nunca es tarde.
Para morir basta un ruidillo.
El de otro corazón al callarse.
No es tarde. ¿Escuchas? En la noche se oye
el siguiente silencio. Mudo, frágil.

FULFILLS

I

Youth keeps its promises, fulfills them.
Ah, what a long word. Wind in leaves.
Fulfills, but invisibly. Smoke in a breeze.
Youth promises. (It lasts. It sleeps.)
Such waking in the night!
But no dawn yet.

II

Once you have seen and heard, you've lived.
One kiss, one pure word. A sound. Two forms.
A meaningless world or shape. Here, hands.
Feel. Feel or kiss. You were asleep.
But don't ever wake.

III

It's not too late. It's never too late.
One little sound is enough to kill you.
The sound of another heart going silent.
It's not too late. Hear it? The silence that follows
sounds in the night. Mute, breakable.

CANCIÓN DEL DÍA NOCHE

Mi juventud fue reina.
Por un día siquiera. Se enamoró de un Norte.
Brújula de la Rosa. De los vientos. Girando.
Se enamoró de un día.

Se fue, reina en las aguas. Azor del aire. Pluma.
Se enamoró de noche. Bajo la mar, las luces.

Todas las hondas luces de luceros hondísimos.
En el abismo estrellas. Como los peces altos.
Se enamoró del cielo, donde pisaba luces.
Y reposó en los vientos, mientras durmió en las olas.
Mientras cayó en cascada, y sonrió, en espumas.

Se enamoró de un orden. Y subvertió sus gradas.
Y si ascendió al abismo, se despeñó a los cielos.

Ay, unidad del día en que, en amor, fue noche.

SONG OF THE NIGHT DAY

My youth was queen.
For a day anyway. It fell in love with a North Star.
A Rose's compass. With the winds. Shifting, turning.
It fell in love with a day.

There it went, ruler of waters. Hawk of the air. Feather.
It fell in love with night. Under the sea, lights.

All the deep lights of the deepest stars.
Stars in the depths. Like fish on high.
It fell in love with the sky, where it walked on lights.
And rested in winds, while it slept in waves.
While it fell in the waterfall, and smiled, in creamy foam.

It fell in love with an order. And undermined it.
And when it climbed the abyss, it threw down the skies.

O, oneness of the day when, in love, it was night.

UN TÉRMINO

Conocer no es lo mismo que saber.
Quien aprendió escuchando; quien padeció o gozó;
quien murió a solas.
Todos andan o corren, mas van despacio siempre
en el viento veloz que ahí los arrastra.
Ellos contra la corriente nadan, pero retroceden,
y en las aguas llevados, mientras se esfuerzan cauce arriba,
a espaldas desembocan.
Es el final con todo en que se hunden.
Mar libre, la mar oscura en que descansan.

A TERM

Understanding is not the same as knowing.
Who learned listening; who suffered or savored;
who died all alone.
Everyone walks or runs, but always slowly
in the fast wind dragging them along.
They swim upstream, but backward,
and in the headwaters, struggling against the current,
they flow out on their backs.
It is the end with everything pulling them down.
Wild ocean, dark ocean where they come to rest.

SIN FE

Tienes ojos oscuros.
Brillos allí que oscuridad prometen.
Ah, cuán cierta es tu noche,
cuán incierta mi duda.
Miro al fondo la luz, y creo a solas.

A solas pues que existes. Existir es vivir con ciencia a ciegas.
Pues oscura te acercas
y en mis ojos más luces
siéntense sin mirar que en ellos brillen.

No brillan, pues supieron.
¿Saber es conocer? No te conozco y supe.
Saber es alentar con los ojos abiertos.
¿Dudar…? Quien duda existe. Sólo morir es ciencia.

FAITHLESS

You have dark eyes.
Glimmers in there that promise darkness.
Ah, how true your night,
how false my doubt.
I see light in the depth, and I believe alone.

Alone since you exist. Existing is living and knowing in the
dark.
Since you approach darkly
and in my eyes more lights
can be felt without seeing they shine in themselves.

They don't shine, since they knew.
Is knowing understanding? I don't know you and I knew.
Knowing is breathing with your eyes open.
Doubt… ? Whoever doubts exists. Only dying is
knowing.

III

QUIEN FUE

La desligada luna se ha fundido
sobre los hombres. El valle entero ha muerto.
La sombra invade su memoria, y polvo
pensado fuera, si existió. Y no ensueño.
Pues mineral la tierra ha anticipado
la materia; el hombre aquí ha aspirado.
Un oro devorado, un viento frío:
ese allegado aliento es una nube.
Quiere durar. No hay piedra. El hombre amaba.

La criatura pensada existe. Mas no basta.
No bastaría. Ah, nunca bastase.
Pensado amor… Si alguien hubo que pudo y que pensara,
alguien de desveladas luces puso
sus ojos en cautela, y soñó un fuego.

Amar no es lumbre, pero su memoria.
Su imaginada lumbre resplandece.
Las movedizas sombras que consume
—delgadas, leves, cual papel ardido—
esa mente voraz que ya no ha visto.
El pensamiento solo no es visible.
Quien ve conoce, quien ha muerto duerme.
Quien pudo ser no fue. Nadie le ha amado.
Hombre que enteramente desdecido, nunca
fuiste creído; ni creado;
ni conocido.
Quien pudo amar no amó. Quien fue, no ha sido.

WHO WAS

The unbound moon has melted
over men. The whole valley has died.
Shadows invade its memory, it might have been
dust of a thought, if it existed. Not a dream.
So mineral earth anticipated
matter; here is what man aspired to.
A squandered gold, an icy wind:
that gathered breath is a cloud.
It wants to last. There is no stone. Man loved.

The thought-of creature exists. But it's not enough.
It wouldn't be enough. There's no way it could ever be
enough.
Thought-of love… If there was someone who could and
who might have thought,
someone up all night with the lights on cleverly
covered his eyes and dreamed of a fire.

Love is not a glow, but its memory.
Its imagined glow is what shines.
The shifty shadows—slender, light,
like paper aflame—consumed
by that ravenous mind that's never seen.
Thought by itself cannot be seen.
Who sees knows; who's died sleeps.
Who could have been wasn't. No one loved him.
A man completely gone to seed, you were never
credible; nor created;
nor comprehended.
Who could have loved did not. Who was, was not.

SUPREMO FONDO

Hemos visto
rostros ilimitados, perfección de otros límites,
una montaña erguida con su perfil clarísimo
y allá la mar, con un barco tan sólo,
bogando en las espinas como olas.

Pero si el dolor de vivir como espumas fungibles
se funda en la experiencia de morir día a día,
no basta una palabra para honrar su memoria,
que la muerte en relámpagos como luz nos asedia.

Pájaros y clamores, soledad de más besos,
hombres que en la muralla como signos imploran.
Y allá la mar, la mar muy seca, cual su seno, y volada.
Su recuerdo son peces putrefactos al fondo.

Lluevan besos y vidas que poblaron un mundo.
Dominad vuestros ecos que repiten más nombres.
Sin memoria las voces nos llamaron, y sordos
o dormidos miramos a los que amar ya muertos.

THE HIGHEST DEPTHS

We've seen
limitless faces, perfection of other limits,
a mountain standing with its lucid profile
and over there the ocean, with just one boat
rowing on the wavelike thorns.

But if the pain of living like fungible foam
is built on the experience of dying day by day,
a word won't suffice to honor its memory,
since death lays siege to us like lightning.

Birds and bells tolling, more kisses' solitude,
men on the wall like signs imploring.
And out there the sea, such a dry sea, like its breast, and
 blown away.
Its memory is fishes rotting in the depths.

Kisses and lives that peopled a world pour down.
Your echoes repeating more names rule over us.
Unremembering voices called to us, and deaf
or asleep we glimpsed our now dead loves.

LOS JÓVENES

I

Unos miran despacio.
Morenos, casi minerales, quietos,
serían vida, cual la piedra, y cantan.
Canta la piedra, canta el que ha vivido.
Los minerales quietos desconocen
qué es muerte, y su moreno ardor gime en la sombra.

Jóvenes son los que despacio pisan. Los hay tristes,
pues la tristeza es juventud, o el beso.
Son numerosos, como los besos mismos, y en el labio
el sol no quema, pero se desposa.
En el carnoso labio vive el día.
La noche pasa en ellos: es sus sombras.
Ellos pasan despacio y roban aura.
La juventud, si quiere, desaloja.
Oh, la absoluta juventud. Son muchos,
son como el mar, y llegan cual la ola.
Sus olas van llegando. Un mar continuo, sin final, aplaca
la sed del arenal o mundo. Y ellos
son aguas lentas, mas seguras,
y quieren
como la arena besa a quien la arrasa.
La mar, la mar. La juventud no ha ardido, mas quemóse.
Y en las arenas queda el agua lúcida.

II

Otros, más invisibles, son quien vive,
quien ríe. Los cuerpos van pasando.
Sólo la luz lo dice. Luz completa,
pues luz poblada. No es el rayo del sol que quema y huye,

THE YOUNG

I

Some look slowly.
Tanned, almost mineral, calm,
they would be life, the same as stone, and sing.
Stone sings, whoever has lived sings.
The calm minerals don't know
what death is, and their dark heat groans in the shadows.

The ones taking those slow steps, they're young. Sad,
since youth is sadness, or a kiss is.
They're countless, like kisses themselves, and their lips
aren't burned by the sun, but it marries them.
Day is alive in those fleshy lips.
Night passes through them: it's their shadows.
They go by slowly, stealing the atmosphere.
Youth, if it wants to, dispossesses.
O absolute youth. So many of them,
they're like the sea, and they arrive in waves.
Their waves keep coming. A perpetual sea, endlessly,
quenches
the beaches' thirst, the world's. And they
are long slow waters, but sure,
and they desire
the same way the sand kisses whoever smooths it.
The sea, the sea. Youth never burned, but it flared out.
And on the sands its lucid water stays.

II

Others, more invisible, are the ones who live,
who laugh. There go their bodies.
The light alone says so. Fulfilled light,
light full of people. It's not the sun's rays that burn and fly
off,

sino el que demorado hay en la carne
con todo el hombre en su ondear luciente.
Toda la vida es luz, y ella se ondula
en el rayo: son las generaciones luminosas
que fueron, pero aún viven, que aún existen.
Y ahí en la luz, hechas la luz, te llegan
como la misma juventud del mundo.

III

Más jóvenes se ven. Son los no muertos,
pues no nacidos.
Son los pensados.
No en la noche o idea,
en el alba, su imagen,
como su pensamiento
están o son. La luz
sigue feliz, ah, no tocada,
pues
quien no nació no mancha. Todas luces,
creídos: oh, pensamiento inmaculado.
Bellos, como el intacto pensamiento solo:
un resplandor.

but the one briefly held in flesh
like everyone else in their glittering swells.
All life is light, and undulates
under the rays; they're the luminous generations
now gone, yet still alive, still existing.
And there in light, made light, they reach you,
touch you like the very youth of the world.

III

You can see more of the young. They're the ones not
dead,
since not yet born.
They're the thought of.
Not in the night or idea,
in the dawn, their image,
like their thought,
they are, they exist. Light
goes happily along, ah, untouched,
since
whoever was never born leaves no trace. Nothing but
light,
believed in: o immaculate thought.
Beautiful, like one whole single thought:
a flash of light.

LUNA POSTRERA

La desdecida luna soñolienta.
La que no supe nunca cómo se llamaba.
Dijo María o Luisa. Reí. Tu nombre es luna.
Luna callada o luna de madera.
Pero luna. Y callóse.
Cómo no, si dormida,
es un pez, un blanco pez limpiado
de todas las memorias, de las espinas tristes,
de su merced doliente. Y duerme
como muerta, en un lago de penas,
pero de penas muy lloradas,
de lágrimas vertidas,
que no son ya dolor, sino agua sola,
agua a solas, sin luces,
como la misma luna muerta.

LAST MOON

The drowsy moon going down.
The one whose name I never knew.
It said María or Luisa. I laughed. Your name is moon.
Quiet moon or wooden moon.
But moon. And it went quiet.
Why not, if asleep
it's a fish, a white fish cleaned
of its memories, its sad thorns,
its grieving mercy. And it sleeps
as if dead, in a lake of sorrows,
but sorrows all sobbed out,
their tears all spilled,
so they're no longer grief, just water,
water alone, lightless,
like the lifeless moon itself.

EL COMETA

La cabellera larga es algo triste.
Acaso dura menos
que las estrellas, si pensadas. Y huye.
Huye como el cometa.
Como el cometa "Haléy" cuando fui niño.
Un niño mira y cree.
Ve los cabellos largos
y mira, y ve la cauda
de un cometa que un niño izó hasta el cielo.

Pero el hombre ha dudado.
Ya puede él ver el cielo
surcado de fulgores.
Nunca creerá, y sonríe.
Sólo más tarde vuelve
a creer y ve sombras.
Desde sus blancos pelos ve negrores,
y cree. Todo lo ciego es ciego,
y él cree. Cree en el luto entero que él tentase.

Así niños y hombres
pasan. El hombre duda.
El viejo sabe. Sólo el niño conoce.
Todos miran correr la cola vívida.

THE COMET

There's something sad about long hair.
Maybe it lasts less long
than stars, if you think about it. And it flies away.
Flies away like a comet.
Like Haley's comet when I was a boy.
A boy sees and believes.
He sees long hair
and looks, and sees the tail
of a comet a boy flung into the sky.

But the man has his doubts.
Now he can see the sky
streaked with fires.
He'll never believe, and he smiles.
Only later does he go back
to believing and he sees shadows.
From his white hair he sees darknesses,
and he believes. Everything blind is blind,
and he believes. He believes in the full bereavement he's
felt.

And that's how boys and men
pass on. The man doubts.
The old man knows. Only the boy understands.
They all watch the flashing tail streak by.

SI ALGUIEN ME HUBIERA DICHO

Si alguna vez pudieras
haberme dicho lo que no dijiste.
En esta noche casi perfecta, junto a la bóveda,
en esta noche fresca de verano.
Cuando la luna ha ardido;
quemóse la cuadriga; se hundió el astro.
Y en el cielo nocturno, cuajado de livideces huecas,
no hay sino dolor,
pues hay memoria, y soledad, y olvido.
Y hasta las hojas reflejadas caen. Se caen, y duran. Viven.

Si alguien me hubiera dicho.
No soy joven, y existo. Y esta mano se mueve.
Repta por esta sombra, explica sus venenos,
sus misteriosas dudas ante tu cuerpo vivo.
Hace mucho que el frío
cumplió años. La luna cayó en aguas.
El mar cerróse, y verdeció en sus brillos.
Hace mucho, muchísimo
que duerme. Las olas van callando.
Suena la espuma igual, sólo a silencio.
Es como un puño triste
y él agarra a los muertos y los explica,
y los sacude, y los golpea contra las rocas fieras.

Y los salpica. Porque los muertos, cuando golpeados,
cuando asestados contra el artero granito,
salpican. Son materia.
Y no hienden. Están aún más muertos,
y se esparcen y cubren, y no hacen ruido.

IF SOMEONE HAD TOLD ME

If only you could have
told me what you didn't say.
On this near-perfect night, under the dome,
on this cool summer night.
When the moon has blazed;
the chariot burned; the star sank.
And in the night sky, curdled with livid hollows,
there's nothing but grief,
since there's memory, and solitude, and forgetting.
And even the reflected leaves are falling. They fall, and
they last. They live.

If someone had told me.
I'm not young, yet I exist. And this hand moves.
It slips snakelike through this darkness, explaining its
venom,
its mysterious doubts before your living body.
The cold's birthday
was long ago. The moon fell into the water.
The ocean closed with green flashes.
It's been asleep
who knows how long. The waves keep hushing.
The spray sounds the same, only silent.
It's like a sad fist
and it grabs the dead and tries to explain them,
and shakes them, and smashes them against the rocks.

And splashes them. Because the dead, smashed,
pounded against the crafty granite,
splash. They're matter.
And they don't stink. They're even more dead,
and they're scattered and spread and they don't make a
sound.

Son muertos acabados.
Quizás aún no empezados.
Algunos han amado. Otros hablaron mucho.
Y se explican. Inútil. Nadie escucha a los vivos.
Pero los muertos callan con más justos silencios.
Si tú me hubieras dicho.
Te conocí y he muerto.
Sólo falta que un puño,
un miserable puño me golpee,
me enarbole y me aseste,
y que mi voz se esparza.

They're dead and gone.
Maybe not even begun.
Some of them loved. Others talked a lot.
And they explain themselves. Pointlessly. Nobody listens
to the living.
But the dead keep quiet with truer silences.
If only you'd told me.
I knew you and I died.
All that's missing is a fist,
a miserable fist to pound me,
to lift me up and smash me,
and scatter my voice.

INTERMEDIO

INTERMISSION

CONOCIMIENTO DE RUBÉN DARÍO

Los ojos callan.
La consumida luz del día ha cejado
y él mira el resplandor. Al fondo, límites.
Los imposibles límites del día,
que él podría tentar. Sus "manos de marqués"
carnosas son, henchidas de materia
real. Miran y reconocen, pues que saben.
Al fondo está el crepúsculo.
Poner en su quemar las manos es saber
mientras te mueves, mientras te consumes.
Como supiste, las ponías,
tus manos naturales,
en la luz no carnal que el alba piensa.

A esa luz más brillaron tus ojos fugitivos,
llegaderos del bien, del mundo amado.
Pues tú supiste que el amor no engaña.
Amar es conocer. Quien vive sabe.
Sólo porque es sapiencia fuiste vivo.

Todo el calor del mundo ardió en el labio.
Grueso labio muy lento, que rozaba
la vida; luego se alzó: la vida allí imprimida.
Por un beso viviste, mas de un cosmos.
Tu boca supo de las aguas largas.
De la escoria y su llaga. También allí del roble.
La enorme hoja y su silencio vivo.
Cual del nácar. Tritón; el labio sopla.

Pero el mar está abierto. Sobre un lomo bogaste.
Delfín ligero con tu cuerpo alegre.
Y nereidas también. Tu pecho una ola,
y tal rodaste sobre el mundo. Arenas…

KNOWING RUBÉN DARÍO

The eyes are quiet.
The consumed daylight has withdrawn
and he regards the afterglow. In the background, boundaries.
The day's impossible limits,
which he would test. His "marquis's hands"
are meaty, packed with real
matter. They look and recognize, because they know.
Dusk in the background.
To place your hands in its blaze is to know
while you're moved, while you're consumed.
As you knew, you put them,
your natural hands,
into the fleshless light the dawn imagines.

Your fleeting eyes shone brighter in that light,
just come from the good, from the loved world.
Because you knew it: love doesn't deceive.
To love is to understand. Whoever lives knows.
Only because of wisdom were you alive.

All the heat in the world burned in your lips.
Your long thick lips that slowly grazed
on life; life rose up and left its imprint there.
You lived for a kiss, but also a cosmos.
Your mouth knew the long waters.
The burnt slag, and also the oak.
The enormous leaf and its living silence.
Like mother of pearl. Triton; the lips blow.

But the ocean is open. You rowed on its back.
A light dolphin in your happy body.
And Nereids too. Your chest a wave,
and rolling across the world. Beaches…

Rubén que un día con tu brazo extenso
batiste espumas o colores. Miras.
Quien mira ve. Quien calla ya ha vivido.
Pero tus ojos de misericordia,
tus ojos largos que se abrieron poco
a poco; tus nunca conocidos ojos bellos,
miraron más, y vieron en lo oscuro.
Oscuridad es claridad. Rubén segundo y nuevo.
Rubén erguido que en la bruma te abres
paso. Rubén callado que al mirar descubres.
Por dentro hay luz. Callada luz, si ardida,

quemada. La dulce quemazón no cubrió toda
tu pupila. La ahondó.
                                        Quien a ti te miró conoció un mundo.
No músicas o ardor, no aromas fríos,
sino su pensamiento amanecido
hasta el color. Lo mismo que en la rosa la mejilla
está. Así el conocimiento está en la uva
y su diente. Está en la luz el ojo.
Como en el manantial la mar completa.

Rubén entero que al pasar congregas
en tu bulto el ayer, llegado, el hoy
que pisas, el mañana nuestro.
Quien es, miró hacia atrás y ve lo que esperamos.
El que algo dice dice todo, y quien
calla está hablando. Como tú que dices
lo que dijeron y ves lo que no han visto
y hablas lo que oscuro dirán. Porque sabías.
Saber es conocer. Poeta claro. Poeta duro.
Poeta real. Luz, mineral y hombre:
todo, y solo.
                        Como el mundo está solo,
y él nos integra.

Rubén who one day reached out your arm
and baptized spray or colors. You look.
Whoever looks sees. Whoever's quiet has lived already.
But your sympathetic eyes,
your wide eyes that were opened little
by little; your never-known beautiful eyes
looked more, and they saw deep into the dark.
Darkness is brightness. Rubén the second and the new,
Rubén proud to stride out into the spray.
Rubén quiet as you look and discover.
There's light inside; quiet light, though burning,

burnt. The sweet blaze didn't cover your whole
pupil. It deepened it.
                                        Whoever looked at you met a world.
No music or passion, no cold aromas,
but its thought dawning
into color. The same way a cheek is revealed
in a rose. The way knowledge is in the bitten
grape. The eye is inside the light.
As in the stream the whole ocean.

Rubén complete who in passing gathers
in your bundle yesterday, arrived, today
where you walk, and our tomorrow.
Whoever is, looked back and sees what we're waiting for.
Whoever says something says everything, and whoever
keeps quiet is speaking. Like you who say
what they said and see what they never saw
and speak what they'll say obscurely. Because you knew.
Knowing is understanding. Bright poet. Hard poet.
Real poet. Light, mineral and man:
everything, and alone.
                                        The way the world is alone,
and includes us.

IV

ALGO CRUZA

La juventud engaña
con veraces palabras. Después son hechos,
acción, el aire; un gesto. Sólo luna a deshoras.

Obtener lo que obtienes es palabra baldía.
Es lo mismo, y distinto.
Pues al aire ese viento
lo atraviesa, más raudo, siendo el mismo y es otro.
Nadie lo ve y él lleva
palabras, voz, semillas,
rayos de luz, memoria,
restos de hombres crispados
o sus pocas cenizas.
Nada se ve: Es lo mismo. Los que viven respiran
si él pasa, y ahí ignorado,
de su son se alimentan.

SOMETHING'S PASSING

Youth plays tricks
with true words. Later, deeds,
action, air; a look. Just an untimely moon.

To hold what you have is a barren word.
It's the same, and different.
Since that wind slips through
the air, quicker, being the same and something else.
Nobody sees it and it sweeps away
words, voice, seeds,
rays of light, memory,
remains of shaky men
or their few ashes.
Nothing's visible. Same thing. The living breathe
as it passes and, unknowing,
feed on its sound.

FELICIDAD, NO ENGAÑAS

Felicidad, no engañas.
Una palabra fue o sería, y dulce
quedó en el labio. Algo
como un sabor
a miel, quizás
aún más a sal
marina. A agua de mar, o a verde fresco
de la campiña. Quizás a gris robusto
del granito o poder, que allí tentaste.

La gravedad del mundo, está ostensible
ante tus ojos. No, no busques
por tu labio el color rubio del beso
que es miel, con su amargor que puede
sobrevivir. Vivir o no vivir no es ignorar
una verdad. El labio sólo sabe
a su final sabor: memoria,
olvido.

HAPPINESS, YOU DON'T CHEAT

Happiness, you don't cheat.
A word was or would be, and sweetly
it stayed on our lips. Something
like a taste
of honey, or maybe
more like sea
salt. Like seawater, or the fresh green
of the countryside. Maybe the strong gray
of granite or power, which you reached for.

The world's gravity—it's right there
in plain sight. No, you don't search
with your lips for the kiss's ruby color,
which is honey, with its bitterness that can
live on. To live or not isn't not to know
a truth. Our lips alone know
their last taste: memory,
forgetting.

NO LO CONOCE

La juventud no lo conoce, por eso dura, y sigue.
¿A dónde vais? Y sopla el viento, empuja
a los veloces que casi giran y van, van con el viento,
ligeros en el mar: pie sobre espuma.

Vida. Vida es ser joven y no más. Escucha,
escucha… Pero el callado son
no se denuncia
sino sobre los labios de los jóvenes.
En el beso lo oyen. Sólo ellos,
en su delgado oír,
pueden, o escuchan.
Roja pulpa besada que pronuncian.

IT DOESN'T KNOW

Youth doesn't know, and that's why it lasts, and continues.
What's your hurry? And the wind blows, sweeping along
the swift who almost spin and go on, go windswept,
lightly over the sea: feet skimming spray.

Life. Life is being young and nothing else. Listen,
listen... But the silent sound
doesn't denounce itself
except on the lips of the young.
They hear it in kisses. Only they,
in their slim hearing,
can, or listen.
Red kissed pulp they pronounce.

LÍMITES Y ESPEJO

I

No insistas. La juventud no engaña. Brilla a solas.
En un pecho desnudo muere el día.
No son palabras las que a mí me engañan.
Sino el silencio puro que aquí nace.
En tus bordes. La silenciosa línea te limita.
Pero no te reduce. Oh, tu verdad latiendo aquí en espacios.

II

Sólo un cuerpo desnudo enseña bordes.
Quien se limita existe. Tú en la tierra.
Cuán diferente tierra se descoge
y se agrupa y reluce y, suma, enciéndese,
carne o resina, o cuerpo, alto, latiendo,
llameando. Oh, si vivir es consumirse, ¡muere!

III

Pero quien muere nace, y aquí aún existes.
¿La misma? No es un espejo un rostro aunque repita
su gesto. Quizá su voz. En el espejo hiélase una imagen
de un sonido. ¡Cómo en el vidrio el labio dejó huellas!
El vaho tan sólo de lo que tú amaras.

LIMITS AND MIRROR

I

Don't argue. Youth doesn't cheat. It shines alone.
The day goes down in a naked chest.
It's not words playing tricks on me.
But the pure silence born here.
At your edges. The silent line is your limit.
But you're not reduced. Oh, your truth beating between
the lines.

II

Only a naked body teaches limits.
Whoever is limited exists. You on earth.
What a different earth spreads out
and gathers and glistens and, finally, ignites,
flesh or resin, or body, exalted, beating,
blazing. Oh, if living is being consumed in flames, die!

III

But whoever dies is born, and here you still exist.
Same thing? A face is not a mirror even if it mimics
its look. Maybe its voice. In the mirror an image of a
sound
is frozen. See how the lips left prints on the glass!
The only breath of what you might have loved.

ROSTRO TRAS EL CRISTAL
(MIRADA DEL VIEJO)

O tarde o pronto o nunca.
Pero ahí tras el cristal el rostro insiste.
Junto a unas flores naturales la misma flor se muestra
en forma de color, mejilla, rosa.
Tras el cristal la rosa es siempre rosa.
Pero no huele.
La juventud distante es ella misma.
Pero aquí no se oye.

Sólo la luz traspasa el cristal virgen.

FACE BEHIND THE WINDOW
(THE OLD MAN'S GAZE)

Late or soon or never.
But there behind the glass the face insists.
Next to some fresh flowers the same flower shows itself
in the shape of a color, a cheek, a rose.
But it has no scent.
Youth in the distance is still itself.
But here we can't hear it.

Light alone can pass through the virgin glass.

ESPERAS

Una ciudad al fondo aguarda un viento.
Pasas en él. Quien se ve engaña,
quien no mira conoce.
Mucho mirar fue luz: ciegos tus ojos.

Calla. La sombra avanza. Es la ciudad dormida aún en más
sueño.
Polvo nocturno, y ojos,
ojos en esa niebla oscura. Arriba, noche.
Calla. La soledad tendida también duerme.
Solo, desnudo,
esperas.

YOU WAIT

A city in the background awaits a wind.
You pass with it. Whoever sees is deceived,
who doesn't look knows.
That long look was light: your eyes blinded.

Quiet. Here comes the dark. It's the city asleep even
  deeper in its dreams.
Night's dust, and eyes,
eyes in that dark fog. Above, night.
Quiet. Solitude stretched out also sleeps.
Alone, naked,
you wait.

LLUEVE

En esta tarde llueve, y llueve pura
tu imagen. En mi recuerdo el día se abre. Entraste.
No oigo. La memoria me da tu imagen sólo.
Sólo tu beso o lluvia cae en recuerdo.
Llueve tu voz, y llueve el beso triste,
el beso hondo,
beso mojado en lluvia. El labio es húmedo.
Húmedo de recuerdo el beso llora
desde unos cielos grises
delicados.
Llueve tu amor mojando mi memoria,
y cae y cae. El beso
al hondo cae. Y gris aún cae
la lluvia.

IT'S RAINING

This afternoon it's raining, and it pours
your image. In my memory the day opens. You walked
in.
I don't hear a thing. Memory gives me just your image.
Only your kiss or rain falls in what I remember.
It rains your voice, and rains your sad kiss,
your deep kiss,
your kiss drenched in rain. Your lips are wet.
Wet with memory our kisses are crying
out of a delicate gray
sky.
It's raining your love soaking my memory,
falling and falling. Kisses
fall into the depths. And the gray rain
keeps falling.

PERO NACIDO

Quien miró y quien no vio.
Quien amó a solas.
La juventud latiendo entre las manos.
Como una ofrenda para un árbol muerto.
Para un dios muerto, o más,
para un dios insepulto.
Quien padeció y gozó, quien miró a solas.
Quien vio y no comprendió

Porque quien vio y miró, no nació. Y vive.

BUT BORN

Who looked and who never saw.
Who loved alone.
Youth beating between their hands.
Like an offering for a dead tree.
For a dead god, or worse,
for a god unburied.
Who suffered and enjoyed, who looked alone.
Who saw and never understood.

Because who saw and looked was never born. And lives.

EL POETA SE ACUERDA DE SU VIDA

Vivir, dormir, morir: soñar acaso.
HAMLET

Perdonadme: he dormido.
Y dormir no es vivir. Paz a los hombres.
Vivir no es suspirar o presentir palabras que aún nos vivan.
¿Vivir en ellas? Las palabras mueren.
Bellas son al sonar, mas nunca duran.
Así esta noche clara. Ayer cuando la aurora,
o cuando el día cumplido estira el rayo
final, y da en tu rostro acaso.
Con un pincel de luz cierra tus ojos.
Duerme.
La noche es larga, pero ya ha pasado.

THE POET SETTLES ACCOUNTS WITH HIS LIFE

To live, to sleep, to die: perchance to dream.
HAMLET

Forgive me: I've been asleep.
And sleeping isn't living. Peace be with you.
Living isn't breathing or prehearing words that might still keep us alive.
Live in them? Words die.
They sound lovely, but they never last.
Just like this clear night. Yesterday when dawn
or when day's end spreads out its last
ray of light, and maybe sets in your face.
With a fine brush of light it paints shut your eyes.
Sleep.
The night is long, but now it's gone.

CUEVA DE NOCHE

Míralo. Aquí besándote, lo digo. Míralo.
En esta cueva oscura, mira, mira
mi beso, mi oscuridad final que cubre en noche
definitiva
tu luminosa aurora
que en negro
rompe, y como sol dentro de mí me anuncia
otra verdad. Que tú, profunda, ignoras.
Desde tu ser mi claridad me llega toda
de ti, mi aurora funeral que en noche se abre.
Tú, mi nocturnidad que, luz, me ciegas.

CAVE AT NIGHT

Look. Kissing you here, I say it. Look.
In this dark cave, look, look
at my kiss, my final darkness covering in definitive
night
your luminous dawn
breaking
into blackness, and like a sun inside me announces
another truth. Which you, so deep, don't know.
Out of your being my clarity comes entirely
from you, my funeral dawn opening into night.
You, my nocturnity made of light, which blinds me.

AMOR IDO

Pulcra fue aquí la luz: un cuerpo acaso.
Amé como a unos rayos, y destellos los besos, muertos
dieron.
Pues quien recuerda acalla
un son, mas no otros brillos.
En el silencio aún luz, y ella no ceja.

No es lo mismo más besos,
más palabras crueles,
que el silencio heredado, que aún se escucha.
Frágil, tenso. ¿Es azul? Cielo. Y son nubes.
Blancas nubes sin paz que heridas cruzan.

LOVE, GONE

The light was lovely here: a body perhaps.
I loved a few rays of light, and glimmering kisses, dead on
arrival.
Since whoever remembers silences
a sound, but no other gleamings.
In silence there's still light, and it doesn't blink.

More kisses, more cruel words,
aren't the same thing
as the hand-me-down silence I can still hear.
Fragile, tense. Is it blue? Sky. And they're clouds.
White peaceless clouds that float by, wounded.

LOS MUERTOS

Ma guarda e passa.
DANTE

Los ojos negros, como los azules.
Como los verdes vivos. Todos hoy, cerrados,
duermen. Su luz ahora sofoca
su rayo mineral. El cielo es alto,
y frío. Más fríos aún, los rostros no contemplan,
o no arrojan verdad. Mas no hay otra verdad que aquí,
dormidos,
los bultos miserables. Calla, y pasa.

THE DEAD

Ma guarda e passa.
DANTE

Black eyes, like blue ones.
Like living green ones. Today, all shut,
asleep. Their mineral shine now smothers
their light. The sky is high,
and cold. Colder still, the faces don't think,
throw off no truth. But there's no other truth than here,
asleep,
the poor lumps. Be quiet, and pass by.

CERCANO A LA MUERTE

No es la tristeza lo que la vida arrumba
o acerca, cuando los pasos muchos son, y duran.
Allá el monte, aquí la vidriada ciudad,
o es un reflejo de ese sol larguísimo
que urde respuestas
a distancia
para los labios que, viviendo, viven,
o recuerdan.
La majestad de la memoria es aire
después, o antes. Los hechos son suspiro.
Ese telón de sedas amarillas
que un soplo empuja, y otra luz apaga.

NEAR DEATH

It isn't sadness life casts off
or pulls close to, when there are so many footsteps, and they
last.
Over there's the mountain, here the glass city,
or it's a reflection of that long, long sun
weaving replies
in the distance
for lips that, living, live
or remember.
The majesty of memory is air
after, or before. Facts are a breath.
That curtain of yellow silk
a breeze lifts up, and another light puts out.

AYER

Ese telón de sedas amarillas
que un sol aún dora y un suspiro ondea.
En un soplo el ayer vacila, y cruje.
En el espacio aún es, pero se piensa
o se ve. Dormido quien lo mira no responde,
pues ve un silencio, o es un amor dormido.

Dormir, vivir, morir. Lenta la seda cruje diminuta,
finísima, soñada: real. Quien es es signo,
una imagen de quien pensó, y ahí queda.
Trama donde el vivir se urdió despacio, y hebra a hebra
quedó, para el aliento en que aun se agita.

Ignorar es vivir. Saber, morirlo.

YESTERDAY

That yellow silk curtain
the sun still shines on and a breath billows.
With a sigh yesterday waves, and rustles.
It's still in space, but it imagines
or sees itself. Asleep the one who sees it doesn't respond,
since he sees a silence, or a sleeping love.

To sleep, to live, to die. Slowly the silk rustles slightly,
so subtly, dreamy: real. Whoever is, is a sign,
an image he dreamed up, and there he is.
A fabric where living was slowly woven, and thread by
   thread
remained, for the breath where it still stirs.

Not knowing is living. Knowing, dying.

V

BESO PÓSTUMO

Así callado, aún mis labios en los tuyos,
te respiro. O sueño en vida o hay vida.
La sospechada vida está en el beso
que vive a solas. Sin nosotros, luce.
Somos su sombra. Porque él es cuerpo cuando ya no estamos.

POSTHUMOUS KISS

Quiet like this, my lips still on yours,
I breathe you. It's either a living dream or we're alive.
The life we can sense is in the kiss
that lives on, alone. Without us, it shines.
We are its shadow. Because it is our bodies when we're
gone.

EL LÍMITE

Basta. No es insistir mirar el brillo largo
de tus ojos. Allí, hasta el fin del mundo.
Miré y obtuve. Contemplé, y pasaba.
La dignidad del hombre está en su muerte.
Pero los brillos temporales ponen
color, verdad. La luz pensada, engaña.
Basta. En el caudal de luz—tus ojos—puse
mi fe. Por ellos vi, viviera.
Hoy que piso mi fin, beso estos bordes.
Tú, mi limitación, mi sueño. ¡Seas!

THE LIMIT

Enough. I'm not still trying to look into the long gleam
in your eyes. To be there until the world ends.
I looked and I took. I thought and I passed.
Man's dignity is in his death.
But the gleams in time give
color, truth. The light of thought plays tricks.
Enough. In the flow of light—your eyes—I placed
my faith. Through them I saw, and may even have lived.
Now that I'm taking my last steps, I kiss these limits.
You, my boundary, my dream. Keep being!

QUIEN HACE VIVE

La memoria de un hombre está en sus besos.
Pero nunca es verdad memoria extinta.
Contar la vida por los besos dados
no es alegre. Pero más triste es darlos sin memoria.
Por lo que un hombre hizo cuenta el tiempo.
Hacer es vivir más, o haber vivido,
o ir a vivir. Quien muere vive, y dura.

WHOEVER DOES, LIVES

A man's memory lives in his kisses.
But a dead memory is never true.
To count one's life by the kisses given
isn't a happy thing. But it's even sadder to give them and
not remember.
Time only counts for what a man has done.
To do is to live more, or to have lived,
or be going to live. Whoever dies lives, and lasts.

SUEÑO IMPURO

Vana verdad de un cuerpo aún insistente.
Ojos negros. Más luz. Cristales. Viso.
Cuando el ocaso se hunde en noche puédese
ignorar otros ojos. Negros son noche, y como noche ciegan.
Pero la noche es nada: sueño, impuro
pues hay un aliento vivo aún en sus bordes.
Las tenebrosas ondas solicitan.
No veo, nada sé. El alba, o nunca.

IMPURE DREAM

Vain truth of a body still persisting.
Black eyes. More light. Windows. Gleams.
When sunset sinks into night you have to be able
to ignore other eyes. They're night black, and like night
they blind.
But night is nothing: a dream, impure
since there's a live breath still at its edges.
The dark waves come courting.
I can't see, know nothing. Dawn, or never.

PERMANENCIA

Demasiado triste para decirlo.
Los árboles engañan. Mientras en brillo sólo van las aguas.
Sólo la tierra es dura.

Pero la carne es sueño
si se la mira, pesadilla si se la siente.
Visión si se la huye.
Piedra si se la sueña.

Calla junto a la roca, y duerme.

PERMANENCE

Too sad to say it.
Trees deceive. While water sparkles on.
Only the earth is hard.

But flesh is a dream,
seen; a nightmare, felt.
A vision, fled.
A stone, dreamed.

Be quiet beside the rock, and sleep.

OTRA VERDAD

La volubilidad
del viento anuncia
otra
verdad. Escucho aún, y nunca,
ese silbo inaudito
en la penumbra.
Oh, calla:
escucha.
Pero el labio está quieto
y no modula
ese sonido misterioso que oigo
en el nivel del beso. Luzca,
luzca tu labio su tibieza o rayos
del sol que al labio mudo asustan,
como otra boca ciega.
Ah, sed impura
de la luz, sed viva o muerta, en boca
última.

ANOTHER TRUTH

The talkative
wind announces
another
truth. I'm still and never listening
for that unhearable whistling
in the dark.
Oh be quiet:
listen.
But your lips are quiet
and don't modulate
that mysterious sound I hear
in the kiss's depths. Light,
light up your lips with its warmth or sun-
beams that frighten the speechless,
like another blind mouth.
Ah, impure thirst
for light, thirst living or dead, in the last
mouth.

EL ENTERRADO

La tierra germinal acepta el beso
último. Este reposo en brazos de quien ama
sin tregua, conforta el corazón. Vida, tú empiezas.
Sábana de verdad que cubre el alma
dormida, mientras los brazos grandes no desmayan
jamás. Tenaz vivo del todo,
bajo un cielo inmediato: tierra, estrellas.

THE BURIED ONE

Germinal earth accepts the final
kiss. This repose in the arms of one who loves
tirelessly, comforts the heart. Life, you're beginning.
Sheet of truth that covers the sleeping
soul, while the great arms never lose heart,
ever. I'm living fiercely, to the hilt,
under an urgent sky: earth, stars.

DESEO FANTASMA

(ADVENIMIENTO DE LA AMADA)

El labio rojo no es rastro de la aurora tenaz, pues huyó,
y queda.
¿Los dientes blancos huella de un beso son?
Espuma, o piedra.
La liviandad de un aire casi puede
deshacerse. Nunca te vi.

—Pues tenla.

PHANTOM DESIRE

(ADVENT OF THE BELOVED)

Red lips are not the trace of a stubborn dawn, since they
fled, and stay.
Are white teeth the tracks of a kiss?
Sea spray, or stone.
The lightness of an air can almost
melt away. I never saw you.

—So hold on.

TIENES NOMBRE

Tu nombre,
pues lo tienes. Toda mi vida ha sido eso:
un nombre. Porque lo sé no existo.
Un nombre respirado no es un beso.
Un nombre perseguido sobre un labio
no es el mundo, pero su sueño a ciegas.
Así bajo la tierra, respiré la tierra.
Sobre tu cuerpo respiré la luz.
Dentro de ti nací: por eso he muerto.

YOU HAVE A NAME

Your name,
since you have one. My whole life was that:
a name. Because I know I don't exist.
A name breathed is not a kiss.
A name pursued on lips
is not the world, but its dream in the dark.
So under the earth, I breathed earth.
Over your body I breathed light.
Inside you I was born: that's why I died.

NOMBRE O SOPLO

Mi nombre fue un sonido
por unos labios. Más que un soplo de aire fue su sueño.
¿Sonó? Como un beso pensado ardió, y quemóse.

¡Qué despacio, sin humos, pasa el viento!

NAME OR BREATH

My name was a sound
between some lips. Its dream was more than a breath.
Did it sound? It burned like a kiss in the mind, and was
consumed.

How slowly, and smokeless, the wind goes by!

FONDO CON FIGURA

Unos dicen que el viento.
Otros alzan papel. La orden. Silencio.
Pero el mar en la costa sí es perpetuo.

La montaña es ceniza. Vedla ardiendo.
Sufre la vida. Callan más los muertos.
Desborda de la copa el pensamiento.

Todo es silencio en la llanura. ¿Hay sueño,
o ensueño? Alerta el mineral; el cielo, suelo.
Despacio, pasa el muerto.

BACKGROUND WITH FIGURE

Some say wind.
Others bring up paper. Order. Silence.
But the ocean along the coast is what goes on forever.

The mountains are ashes. Watch them burn.
Life suffers. The dead get quieter.
Thought's cup runs over.

All quiet on the plain. A dream,
or fantasy? Vigilant minerals; sky, soil.
Slowly, there goes the dead man.

PRESENTE, DESPUES

Basta. Tras la vida, no hay beso y yo te siento.
Tus fenecidos labios me sugieren
que vivo. O soy yo quien te llama.
Poner los labios en tu idea es sentirte
proclamación. Oh, sí, terrible, existes.
Soy quien finó, quien pronunció tu nombre, como forma
mientras moría.

De mí nacida;
aquí presente porque yo te he dicho.

PRESENT, LATER

Enough. There's no kiss after life, but I can feel you.
Your finished lips hinted
that I'm alive. Or I'm the one calling you.
To place my lips on the idea of you is to feel you
as a proclamation. O yes, you exist, terribly.
I'm the finished one, who spoke your name, like a rite,
while I was dying.

Born of me;
here because I said you.

PENSAMIENTOS FINALES

Nació y no supo. Respondió y no ha hablado.

Las sorprendidas ánimas te miran
cuando no pasas. El viento nunca cumple.
Tu pensamiento a solas cae despacio.
Como las fenecidas hojas caen y vuelven
a caer, si el viento las dispersa.
Mientras la sobria tierra las espera,
abierta. Callado el corazón, mudos los ojos,
tu pensamiento lento se deshace
en el aire. Movido suavemente. Un son de ramas
finales, un desvaído sueño de oros vivos
se esparce… Las hojas van cayendo.

FINAL THOUGHTS

He was born but didn't know. He answered but never spoke.

The surprised spirits watch you
not passing. Wind never keeps its word.
All by itself your thought is slowly falling.
As the dead leaves fall and fall
again, blown about by the wind.
While sober earth, wide open, waits
for them. Heart gone quiet, eyes gone mute,
your slow thoughts dissolve
in the air. Gently rustling. A sound of final
branches, an awkward dream of live gold
scattering… The leaves keep falling.

EL OLVIDO

No es tu final como una copa vana
que hay que apurar. Arroja el casco, y muere.

Por eso lentamente levantas en tu mano
un brillo o su mención, y arden tus dedos,
como una nieve súbita.
Está y no estuvo, pero estuvo y calla.
El frío quema y en tus ojos nace
su memoria. Recordar es obsceno;
peor: es triste. Olvidar es morir.

Con dignidad murió. Su sombra cruza.

OBLIVION

Your end is not some vain wineglass
that needs to be drunk dry. Throw down the cask, and die.

That's why you slowly raise in your hand
a glimmer or its hint, and your fingers burn
like a blizzard.
It is and it wasn't, but it was and it's not talking.
Cold burns and in your eyes its memory
is born. Remembering is obscene;
worse: it's sad. Forgetting is dying.

He died with dignity. There goes his shadow.

A NOTE ON THE AUTHOR

Vicente Aleixandre, born in Seville in 1898, was one of the leading figures of Spain's fabled Generation of 1927. Due to his fragile health, he remained in Spain after the civil war to become the resident link to that cohort of poets, encouraging and mentoring younger writers through personal meetings and postal correspondence. Author of more than a dozen volumes of poetry and several of prose, he was awarded the Nobel Prize for literature in 1977. His selected poems in English, *A Longing for the Light,* was published in the United States in 1978. Vicente Aleixandre died in Madrid in 1984.

A NOTE ON THE TRANSLATOR

Stephen Kessler is a poet, prose writer, translator, and editor. His other recent books include *Scratch Pegasus* (poems), *The Tolstoy of the Zulus* (essays), *The Mental Traveler* (novel), and *The Sonnets* by Jorge Luis Borges (as editor and principal translator). His version of *Desolation of the Chimera* by Luis Cernuda received the Harold Morton Landon Translation Award from the Academy of American Poets, and his translation of Cernuda's collected prose poems, *Written in Water,* received a Lambda Literary Award. He lives in California where he edits *The Redwood Coast Review*. For more about Stephen Kessler, visit www.stephenkessler.com.

TITLES FROM BLACK WIDOW PRESS

TRANSLATION SERIES

A Life of Poems, Poems of a Life
by Anna de Noailles. Translated by Norman R. Shapiro. Introduction by Catherine Perry.

Approximate Man and Other Writings
by Tristan Tzara. Translated and edited by Mary Ann Caws.

Art Poétique
by Guillevic. Translated by Maureen Smith.

The Big Game
by Benjamin Péret. Translated with an introduction by Marilyn Kallet.

Capital of Pain
by Paul Eluard. Translated by Mary Ann Caws, Patricia Terry, and Nancy Kline.

Chanson Dada: Selected Poems
by Tristan Tzara. Translated with an introduction and essay by Lee Harwood.

Essential Poems and Writings of Joyce Mansour: A Bilingual Anthology
Translated with an introduction by Serge Gavronsky.

Essential Poems and Prose of Jules Laforgue
Translated and edited by Patricia Terry.

Essential Poems and Writings of Robert Desnos: A Bilingual Anthology
Edited with an introduction and essay by Mary Ann Caws.

EyeSeas (Les Ziaux) by Raymond Queneau. Translated with an introduction by Daniela Hurezanu and Stephen Kessler.

Furor and Mystery & Other Writings
by René Char. Edited and translated by Mary Ann Caws and Nancy Kline.

The Inventor of Love & Other Writings
by Gherasim Luca. Translated by Julian and Laura Semilian. Introduction by Andrei Codrescu. Essay by Petre Răileanu.

La Fontaine's Bawdy
by Jean de La Fontaine. Translated with an introduction by Norman R. Shapiro.

Last Love Poems of Paul Eluard
Translated with an introduction by Marilyn Kallet.

Love, Poetry (L'amour la poésie)
by Paul Eluard. Translated with an essay by Stuart Kendall.

Poems of André Breton: A Bilingual Anthology
Translated with essays by Jean-Pierre Cauvin and Mary Ann Caws.

Poems of A. O. Barnabooth
by Valéry Larbaud. Translated by Ron Padgett and Bill Zavatsky.

Poems of Consummation by Vicente Aleixandre. Translated by Stephen Kessler

Préversities: A Jacques Prévert Sampler
Translated and edited by Norman R. Shapiro.

The Sea and Other Poems
by Guillevic. Translated by Patricia Terry. Introduction by Monique Chefdor.

To Speak, to Tell You? Poems by Sabine Sicaud.
Translated by Norman R. Shapiro. Introduction and notes by Odile Ayral-Clause.

LITERARY THEORY / BIOGRAPHY SERIES

Revolution of the Mind: The Life of André Breton
by Mark Polizzotti. Revised and augmented.

LOUISIANA HERITAGE SERIES (forthcoming)

Jules Choppin (1830–1914)
New Orleans Poems in Creole and French
Translated by Norman R. Shapiro.

MODERN POETRY SERIES

An Alchemist with One Eye on Fire
by Clayton Eshleman

Anticline by Clayton Eshleman

Archaic Design by Clayton Eshleman

Backscatter: New and Selected Poems
by John Olson

The Caveat Onus
by Dave Brinks. The complete cycle, four volumes in one.

City Without People: The Katrina Poems
by Niyi Osundare

Concealments and Caprichos
by Jerome Rothenberg

Crusader-Woman
by Ruxandra Cesereanu. Translated by Adam J. Sorkin. Introduction by Andrei Codrescu.

Curdled Skulls: Poems of Bernard Bador
Translated by the author with Clayton Eshleman.

Endure: Poems by Bei Dao
Translated by Clayton Eshleman and Lucas Klein.

Exile is My Trade: A Habib Tengour Reader
Translated by Pierre Joris.

Fire Exit by Robert Kelly

Forgiven Submarine
by Ruxandra Cesereanu and Andrei Codrescu

from stone this running
by Heller Levinson

The Grindstone of Rapport: A Clayton Eshleman Reader
Forty years of poetry, prose, and translations.

Larynx Galaxy by John Olson

Memory Wing by Bill Lavender

Packing Light: New and Selected Poems
by Marilyn Kallet

The Present Tense of the World: Poems 2000–2009
by Amina Saïd. Translated with an introduction by Marilyn Hacker.

The Price of Experience
by Clayton Eshleman

The Secret Brain: Selected Poems 1995–2012
by Dave Brinks

Signal from Draco: New and Selected Poems
by Mebane Robertson

forthcoming modern poetry titles

ABC of Translation
by Willis Barnstone

An American Unconscious
by Mebane Robertson

Eye of Witness: A Jerome Rothenberg Reader
Edited with commentaries by Heriberto Yepez & Jerome Rothenberg

Memory by Bernadette Mayer

The Love That Moves Us
by Marilyn Kallet